THE CHANGING FACE OF
CARDIFF

THE CHANGING FACE OF
CARDIFF

BRIAN LEE

First published in Great Britain in 2008 by
The Breedon Books Publishing Company Limited
Breedon House, 3 The Parker Centre,
Derby, DE21 4SZ.

This paperback edition published in Great Britain in 2013 by DB Publishing,
an imprint of JMD Media Ltd

ISBN 978-1-78091-333-9

Printed and bound in the UK by Copytech (UK) Ltd Peterborough

CONTENTS

For John Billot
former sports editor of the *Western Mail*
and a real gent.

CHARACTER
The fool to pen will often leap,
While wiser men prefer to sleep.
But wise men do not history make,
Nor sleeping men,the action take.
No, commit your thoughts to words
and pen.
And let your peers judge you then.
For you can say: "I spoke my mind
I am not of the cringing kind."

Anon

AUTHOR'S ACKNOWLEDGEMENTS

I would like to thank all those people who loaned me photographs for this book, and these include: Gerald May, John Smith, Allen Hambly, Richard Shepherd, David Davies, Dennis Pope, Terence Soames, Russell Harvey, Mrs Evans, Associated British Ports, Cardiff Council, Hills Press Agency and Tempest Photography. I also need to thank Tony Woolway, chief librarian at the *Western Mail & Echo* and his colleagues Edwina Turner and Rob Mager for their help and also Katrina Coopey and her staff at the Cardiff Central Library for their assistance. I would also like to thank Rhodri Morgan for writing the foreword for the book.

INTRODUCTION

RT HON RHODRI MORGAN AM

The Changing Face of Cardiff is a fascinating theme for a book, especially for someone like me who was born and brought up in the city – coming towards the end of my seventh decade as a Cardiffian – and who has lived through the massive changes we have seen over the past 20 or 30 years. Sometimes I think to myself what do I miss about the old Cardiff I grew up in and how it was when I first got involved in politics in the 1960s?

I miss those great music venues – scruffy and unscrubbed though they were. I miss the Quebec and the New Moon. The Quebec was a very dingy Docks boozer, but a place where Victor Parker, a great Cardiff Docks chord guitarist, used to produce wonderful music. Music in the Quebec was free, and the Sunday summer lunchtime sessions out in the street frequented by all the most talented singers in the Cardiff area were something to behold. The New Moon was just behind the old fruit market on the Hayes and had the most rickety fire escape you have ever seen, set on a counter-balanced spindle screwed into the pine-end of the wall. You had to go up 50 steps to get in, and here you did have to pay a modest entrance fee to hear the guest musicians, but it was a great music venue. I am grateful that there was never a fire when I was there because if we had had to get out onto that fire escape I am pretty sure it would not have taken our weight and we would all have collapsed onto a heap of rotten oranges and spuds discarded by the market traders in the Hayes open-air fruit market!

I miss the Big Windsor – a great place to eat out once a year with your girlfriend or wife, and such fantastic French food. You wouldn't get better in Paris or London and, of course, it was a quarter of the price. The waitresses were just amazing characters – they weren't French, but they certainly knew their French food. Furthermore, the Windsor gave us the hopeless neurotic chef who had been sacked, went up into the roof space of the Big Windsor, poured cooking oil over everything and set it alight and then jumped out of the window onto a passing double-decker bus. That is a true story, but it is also a part of local folklore because you couldn't have made it up. This is the kind of incident that happened in the old Cardiff, but you can't really imagine it happening today.

That was the Cardiff of the 60s – when I had my baptism in politics and was involved in the fierce rucks and mauls over control of the City Hall and trying to ensure the re-election of the apparently ageless Jim Callahan and George Thomas to the House of Commons. This culminated in the 1970s with the astonishing coincidence of the Prime Minister and the Speaker of the House of Commons both representing adjoining seats in Cardiff.

There was a very romantic era for sport in Cardiff in the 60s too, when Gareth Edwards, Barry John and Gerald Davies came from the west to revive Cardiff's rugby fortunes, while at the same time Cardiff City, having lost their ambitions to play again in the old First Division, concentrated their efforts on the European Cup and defeated Real Madrid and also reached the semi-finals of the UEFA Cup, only to be defeated by SV Hamburg by a single goal. Shades of that era have now re-emerged in 2008 with Cardiff City reaching the FA Cup Final at Wembley.

More recently, the FA Cup Final was held in Cardiff for seven years in a row, from 2000–06, and the city's downtown has leapt forward in the modernisation stakes with the St David's Centre being built, then the Docks turning into the Bay and now St David's Centre 2 emerging to the south of the first St David's Centre. I can hardly let the occasion go by without making some reference to the battle over the barrage which completely dominated the early years of my period in the House of Commons, from 1987–97. The friendships made then have never been broken. The barrage is now in place, the oxygenation system – with those bubblers bubbling away every few yards across the Bay, up the Taff and up the River Ely – has been installed to keep the fish population happy, and the property boom to build luxury apartments around the Bay has come and possibly passed its crest. The key thing is that Cardiff should keep its essential spirit as a city as well as being a very cosmopolitan commercial centre and the capital of Wales.

The essence of the city of Cardiff is its contrasts. As I put it sometimes, it is a long way from Gwaelod Y Garth to Tiger Bay. Actually it is only about seven miles, perhaps less than that as the crow flies, but a city that can incorporate one of the last Welsh-speaking villages in south-east Wales and is Wales's number-one multi-ethnic, multi-faith, multi-cultured, multi-coloured melting pot has got to be one of the world's most interesting cities. It is definitely not one of the world's biggest cities, but it is certainly one of the world's most interesting. That's why its changing face will be of great interest not just to Cardiffians like me, but to people with an interest in city life all over the world.

CHAPTER ONE
BEFORE THE CAMERA

Cardiff's first town hall, which was also known as the Town House, Bothall or Guildhall, was erected halfway along High Street in 1331. It was a two-storey building and the upper floor served as a courtroom and general assembly room. On the ground floor could be found the prison cells, stocks, water pump and the corn and meat market, which was known as the 'Shambles'.

A turret, town bell and clock tower were added much later, but by 1741 the building was in such a bad state of repair that a decision was made to build another town hall on the same site. The new building, which featured a Georgian façade and a double flight of stone steps flanked by an iron balustrade, was opened in 1747. With the increase in the population of Cardiff in the days when coal was king, and the subsequent opening of the Bute Docks, it soon became clear that a much larger town hall was needed.

An acre of land between St Mary Street and Westgate Street, where the Commercial Bank of Wales later stood, was put aside and building commenced in 1849. During the work, earlier walls were found and a circular stairway of great depth, thought to be part of the old town's defences, was also uncovered.

Opened in 1854, the new town hall also housed the old post office, police court and parade ground, as well as the fire brigade offices and rates office.

July 1881. No. 1036.

Cardiff from Clock Tower Looking East.

Cardiff from the castle clock tower looking east, *c.*1881.

Cardiff Free Library,
Museum and School of Arts
and Science, c.1880.

Cardiff Castle's famous clock tower, c.1880.

Cardiff Town Hall. Post Office. &c.

Town Hall, St Mary Street (left of picture), opened in 1854.

The Sailors' Home in
Stuart Street was opened
in 1856.

The Sailors' Home. Bute Docks. Cardiff

Opened in 1866, the Royal
Hotel in St Mary Street was
refurbished in 2001.

Wesleyan Chapel in Loudoun
Place, Cardiff Docklands,
*c.*1880.

The Docks, Cardiff.

'When Coal was King'. A docklands scene, *c.*1880.

Canton near Cardiff.

Cardiff Bridge, which has often mistakenly been called Canton Bridge, *c.*1880.

Llandaff Cathedral, which was bombed during World War Two, *c*.1880.

St John's Church was originally built in the
12th century as a chapel of ease to St Mary's.

The days of the old windjammers – sailing ships – have long passed, *c.*1880.

Cardiff Docks.

Bute Docks.

The Bute West Dock was opened in 1839 and the Bute East Dock in 1855.

The Independent
Chapel in Charles
Street, *c.* 1880.

A romantic etching of Cardiff Castle by J. Newman, *c.* 1880.

Another view of St John's Church, *c.*1880.

A rather Gothic view of Llandaff
Cathedral, *c*.1880.

Llandaff Cathedral

THE NORTH ENTRANCE, (NORTH ROAD) CARDIFF.

The North Entrance, North Road, Kingsway, with St John's Church in the background, *c*.1870.

Chapter Two
POSTCARDS

The Queen's West Shopping Centre, opened in 1987, is now situated where the shops, on the left of the picture, can be seen, c.1903.

Horse and carts were still in vogue when this Queen Street picture postcard was taken, c.1905.

Andrew's Arcade, which used to be to the right of this picture, disappeared in 2007 when the Queen Street shops were refurbished.

Queen Street, *c.*1906.

The Tivoli Hotel was on the extreme right of this picture and closed in 1960.

Seccombes, the building right of the picture, a popular Queen Street department store, closed in 1977.

The building in the centre is the old Empire Theatre, *c.*1907.

The Park Hotel, left of the picture, opened in 1885. It is now part of the Thistle Group.

In 1853 an attempt to change the name of Queen Street to Park Street proved unsuccessful.

The Park Hotel, built in French
Renaissance style, *c.*1905.

High Street by night, *c.*1905.

Various views of Cardiff.
F. Hartmann's miniature
series.

To the extreme right of the picture is the Terminus Hotel, *c.*1905.

The Great Western Hotel is on the left of the picture, *c.*1906.

St Mary Street was named after St Mary's Church, destroyed in the Great Flood of 1607.

To the left of the picture is the
Queen's Hotel in St Mary Street
which closed in 1974.

Barry's Hotel, St Mary Street, is left
of the picture, *c.*1905.

Another view of St Mary Street,
*c.*1906.

The big building to the left of the picture is the Royal Hotel, built in 1866.

The Cardiff Free Library, *c.*1905.

The statue of John Bachelor was unveiled in 1866.

When trams ran along Working
Street.

The Taff Vale railway bridge can be
seen in the background, *c.*1905.

Newport Road, *c.*1905.

University College, Newport Road, *c*.1908.

The old infirmary was at one time situated in this building.

Roath Park has changed a lot since this picture was taken, *c*.1900.

The best way to view St John's Tower is from St Mary Street.

Oliver's shoe shop (left) was situated on the corner of High Street and Church Street for many years.

According to the old 16th-century map of Cardiff, St Mary's Church was as big as St John's Church.

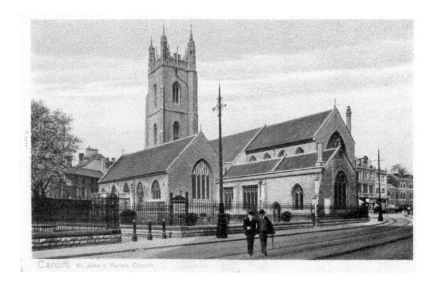

The leafy houses in Cathedral Road were built in the 1890s, and a number of them at the town end of the road were converted into offices in the 1970s.

The Lock House, or Castle Lodge, in North Road was bombed by Germans in March 1941.

The magnificent old Post Office building in Westgate Street was built on the site of Hutchinson's and Tayleur's Wooden Circus Theatre in 1896.

Castle Street, *c.*1905.

A view of the River Taff from Cardiff Bridge.

Another view of the River Taff.

Shops in Romilly Crescent in 1906.

The Royal Infirmary, *c*.1906.

The Law Courts in the Civic Centre.

The Law Courts viewed from
another angle.

A rare postcard of the Civic Centre.

Gorsedd Gardens, Cathays Park.

A romantic view of the City Hall.

The statue of Judge Gwilyn Watkins Williams had yet to be erected when this picture of the Law Courts was taken.

Roath Park Tea House and waterfall, *c.*1900.

Horse-drawn trams were still in vogue when this pictue was taken.

Cardiff Castle.

The City Hall and clock tower.

The New Town Hall, Cardiff. 1186.

The south wing of the castle was rebuilt in 1893.

CARDIFF. THE CASTLE FROM THE GROUNDS,

The animal wall stood in front of the castle when this picture was taken.

The Pier Head building was erected in 1896.

Sailing ships in Cardiff docks.

A general dock scene.

SS *Westonia* and SS *Gwalia* in dock.

The Pier Head building was known as the Bute Dock offices.

The Exchange building can be seen in the background.

An artist's impression of Llandaff Cathedral.

St Paul's Church in Grangetown. The church was consecrated in 1890 by the Bishop of Llandaff.

St Peter's Roman Catholic Church. St Peter's School, left, was demolished in 1981.

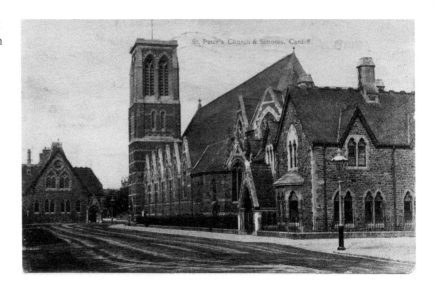

Gorsedd Gardens, Cathays Park.

Sophia Gardens fountain was erected around 1866.

The Cardiff Mercury Motor Inn at Castleton has now been demolished and houses have been built on the site.

Victoria Park was opened on 16 June 1897. It is named after Queen Victoria.

Cardiff's most famous animal, Billy the seal, was placed in Victoria Park lake in 1912. Billy was found dead in the lake in 1939 when it was also discovered that he should have been called Milly.

Roath Park was opened in 1894.

A busy High Street, *c.*1910.

A not-so-busy High Street! This photograph was probably taken on a Sunday.

CHAPTER THREE

A BIRD'S-EYE VIEW

Many Cardiffians used to stand on the wall which surrounded the ruins of Herbert House and look through the iron railings of this once historic site. John Ballinger, in his *Guide to Cardiff*, published 100 years ago, wrote: 'The Grey Friars (Franciscans or Friars Minors) had their house in Crockherbtown, south of the City Hall. After the dissolution the site was aquired by Sir George Herbert, whose grandson, Sir William, built a mansion known as The Friars, a portion of which is still standing, a light handsome structure in Tudor style. The site of Grey Friars was excavated by the Marquis of Bute who had the outlines rebuilt a few feet above the ground. Some graves inside the church were discovered and marked. It was here that Llewellin Bren and his foe, Sir William Fleming, were buried but attempts to identify the graves were not satisfactory.' The remains of Llewellin Bren (or Llywelyn Bren) were said to have been carried to Grey Friars for a Christian burial in 1317 after he had been dragged to a traitor's death for his part in the short-lived Welsh revolt. The Welsh chieftain was allegedly put to death at Cardiff with great barbarity and in direct violation of the King's command. He was drawn by horses, then hanged, his entrails taken out and burned while his limbs were cut off and sent through all Glamorgan to strike terror into other traitors. As for Sir William Fleming, when fortunes changed he was hanged at Cardiff Castle's Black Tower. His tomb, which was made of fair stone, and Llewellin Bren's tomb, said to be made of wood, were apparently still in Grey Friars Church when it was dismantled in 1538. They were thought to have been discovered in 1887 along with the skeletons of men, women and children on the site where the monstrous Pearl Assurance tower, now Capital Towers, stands.

An earlier Cardiff, *c.*1870. One of the few remaining buildings in the city centre is St John's Church.

The Corner House, Cardiff Castle, with its bay window, was demolished in 1877.

Cardiff Bridge looking towards Canton. It collapsed into the River Taff during the floods of 1792.

In the centre of this 1965 picture is Bute Road, which leads to Cardiff Docks, or Cardiff Bay as it is now known.

The world-famous Cardiff Arms Park, which was demolished to make way for the Millennium Stadium, can be seen left of picture, 1962.

Cardiff's magnificent city centre. To the right of the picture, in front of the building known as Magnet House, now demolished, can be seen the ruins of Herbert House in Greyfriars Road.

This was how the city centre looked from the air in 1962. The Glamorgan Canal used to run where all the cars can be seen parked (extreme right of picture).

CHAPTER FOUR
CITY CENTRE

When David Morgan opened his store on The Hayes on 31 October 1879, he couldn't have had any idea that the little draper's shop would one day become one of the city's best-loved landmarks. By 1884 David Morgan had extended his business southwards along The Hayes and a five-storey building was erected. Later, the acquistion of land between the rear of the Royal Arcade and Tabernacle Lane enabled him to increase the depth of his store. When George Hopkins's grocery store became available he acquired this too, and built a second five-storey shop. The St Mary Street store was opened in 1898 and the following year the Morgan Arcade was completed.

It was a sad day for South Walians when David Morgan's family store on The Hayes closed in 2005, as it had provided thousands of customers with unrivalled service for 125 years. This was photographed c.1910.

The Free Library on The Hayes was opened in 1882 and the southern end was completed in 1896.

The statue of John Batchelor (centre) was erected in 1886. This Tuck's postcard reads, 'The public library, which handsome building was recently enlarged, fronts upon a smaller square which on a Saturday is noisy with cheap Jacks and vendors of quack medicines gather round the statue shown, which is that of a local politican.'

The open-air market on The Hayes in 1946.

The Hayes Island Snack Bar has been a popular venue for generations of Cardiffians. It is seen here in 2007.

Plans have been put forward to establish a Cardiff Local History museum in the old Central Library, seen in this picture in 2007.

The statue of John Batchelor (centre) has been moved on several occasions over the years.

The bulldozers get to work and John Batchelor surveys the demolished buildings. In the background can be seen the Central Library, which was opened in 1988 and has now been demolished.

The Capital Exchange shopping complex was built on the site where these cottages once stood in Crockherbtown. The photograph dates from *c.*1883.

The name Crockherbtown was changed to Queen Street in 1886. To the left of the picture can be seen the Empire Theatre, *c.*1910.

The Park Hotel in Queen Street, 1918. Built in French Renaissance style in 1885, it is now part of the Thistle group of hotels.

Queen Street in the 1940s. Specsavers is now situated where the Queen's Cinema can be seen (right of picture).

Trams came to Cardiff in 1902 and these two are seen passing the Olympia Cinema in Queen Street (right of picture), which opened in 1935 and was earlier known as Andrews Hall.

The Aneurin Bevan statue in Queen Street was unveiled by Michael Foot in 1987. This picture was taken in 2002.

A favourite Queen Street haunt for thousands of Cardiffians was the Carlton Hotel (seen left of picture) which was bombed during World War Two.

These people are walking past where once the Empire Theatre, later Gaumont Cinema, and later still where C&A once stood, in 2007.

The people strolling past Specsavers in 2007 probably have no idea that the Queen's Cinema once stood on the site.

The Olympia and Odeon cinemas in Queen Street used to be around where Principles and River Island now stand, 2007.

Queen Street was widened in 1862 and many of the old buildings were demolished.

One of the oldest churches in Cardiff is St John's Church, which was founded at the end of the 12th century.

Some things never seem to change and St John's Church is one of them.

The people seen here in 1887 are standing in North Street, renamed Kingsway in 1909.

These terraced houses on the corner of North Street can be seen in the previous picture.

On the corner of Kingsway and Queen Street, formerly Smith Street, can be seen the Red Lion pub, which stood on the site from 1792 until 1958, *c.*1906.

The underground lavatories seen in the previous picture were still in use when this picture was taken in the 1950s.

The policeman standing in the middle of Duke Street did not have much traffic to worry about in 1921.

The shops to the right of the picture were situated in front of the castle and were demolished in 1923 when the road was widened.

In earlier times, Duke Street was known as Duckstrete, suggesting a place where poultry was sold.

There are no shops in front of the castle to spoil the view in this modern-day picture, taken in 2007.

A postcard scene of St Mary Street in the 1920s.

The southern end of St Mary Street where four pubs – the Royal Oak, Blue Anchor, Elliots Hotel – and The Terminus once stood.

Note the trolleybus overhead wires in this St Mary Street picture.

The Sandringham Hotel can be seen left of picture, *c.*1950.

St Mary Street in the 1950s. The popular Queen's Hotel, left of picture, closed in 1974.

St Mary Street looking towards High Street, 2007.

One of the many courts in the centre of Cardiff was Rowes Square on The Hayes, *c*.1890.

Landore Court stood between the Golate and the Queen's Hotel, *c*.1881.

One of the oldest streets in Cardiff is Womanby Street. In 1270 it was known as Hundemanby. The name is thought to mean 'the home or dwelling of the hound man or keeper of hounds', c.1890.

This picture of Womanby Street was taken in 2007.

The historic Golate runs between St Mary Street and Westgate Street. The *Western Mail & Echo* offices, which had stood right of picture, were demolished when this picture was taken in 1975.

The Golate, an ancient lane, was a no-go area for nearly two years owing to a £4.7 million complex of luxury apartments being built there in 2004.

The buildings to the right of Working Street were demolished to make way for St David's Hall, which was opened by Queen Elizabeth the Queen Mother in 1982.

Westgate Street in the 1880s. The small terraced houses of Temperance Town can be seen in the background. The Cardiff Arms Park was built on the stretch of land to the right of the picture.

Cardiff Bridge in around 1871. It is often mistakenly called Canton Bridge.

The Corner House, which stood in Castle Street, *c.*1876.

The world-famous Cardiff Arms Park is demolished to make way for the Millennium Stadium.

Many people were of the opinion that the Millennium Stadium should have been built outside the city centre.

The Millennium Stadium was a venue for the 1999 Rugby World Cup.

A view of the work being carried out on the corner of Scott Road and Park Street.

The Millennium Stadium begins to take shape.

This was how The Hayes looked during the 1990s.

Walking in the opposite direction, this is how it looked in 2007.

Thomson House in Havelock Street, the home of the *South Wales Echo* and *Western Mail,* was officially opened in 1961 and is now due to be partly demolished and rebuilt.

The bus station in Central Square which is undergoing a makeover.

Wood Street, which was named after a Colonel Wood, who owned land in the area.

St David's House, Wood Street.

The open-air market in Mill Lane moved to Bridge Street in 1981. The New Moon Club used to be situated on the top floor of the warehouse building in the background.

The market in Bridge Street.

The 'new' Cardiff Central Library in St David's Link was officially opened in 1988 and was demolished in 2007 to make way for the £535 million St David's 2 shopping centre.

When this picture of Queen Street Bridge was taken in 1972, a day return to London cost just £3.45.

Queen Street Bridge, June 2007.

The former AA building in Queen Street is now a block of luxury flats.

This is how they looked in June 2007.

Calders, the men's outfitters, used to be on the corner of Queen Street and Churchill Way.

The Capitol Exchange complex is now where Calders and the Savoy Bar once stood.

Queen Street, *c*.1970. The white building in the centre is Barclays Bank, which is still there.

In this picture Barclays Bank is partly obscured by the tree, June 2007.

Arthur Kaltenbach, the watchmaker and jeweller, was in Caroline Street for many years.

Greggs is now situated on the site of Arthur Kaltenbach's shop, June 2007.

Queen Street Station, Station Terrace. The YMCA and Cory Hall buildings (right of picture) were demolished in 1983.

Station Terrace with the Capitol Exchange shopping complex on the right of the picture.

One of the few remaining buildings in the Hills Street area still standing is the old Electricity Board showrooms, seen here *c.*1955.

The former Electricity Board showrooms, now Habitat. The lady in the picture is the author's wife Jacqueline Lee.

CHAPTER FIVE

A VANISHED DOCKLANDS

Cardiff prospered because of the coal trade and at one time it was the largest coal exporting centre in the world. Ship repairing and owning also became a very important industry and Cardiff Docks was capable of accommodating some of the largest ships afloat. To supplement these industries, a number of other ancillary businesses and industries emerged, such as copper works, wagon-building, timber yards and flour mills. The Dowlais Steel Works opened at East Moors in 1891, providing work for thousands of Cardiffians and migrant workers. However, the industrial decline since World War Two has seen great changes in the docklands area of Cardiff now known as Cardiff Bay.

Cardiff Docks in the days when windjammers – sailing ships – ruled the waves.

Designed in French Gothic style, the Pier Head building housed the offices of the Bute Dock Company, *c.*1900.

A more recent picture of the Pier Head building.

The Merchants' Exchange building, Bute Docks, *c*.1930.

An aerial view of Mount Stuart Docks.

The dash for the South Pole and the *Terra Nova* sails out of Cardiff Docks, 15 June 1910.

Cardiff Docks used to be Britain's largest coal-exporting port.

Dockers stacking raw sugar by electric escalators at the Queen Alexandra Dock, *c.*1960.

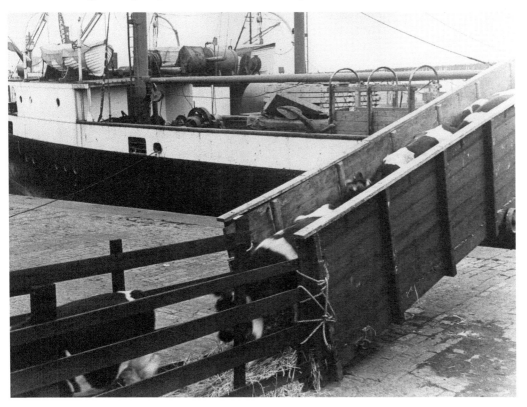

Landing Dutch cattle from the SS *Orestes* at Roath Dock, October 1947.

Discharging a cargo of meat to King's Wharf Cold Store, *c.*1955.

A cargo of frozen meat being discharged from the SS *Port Jackson*, March 1944.

A 60-ton floating crane in action, October 1943.

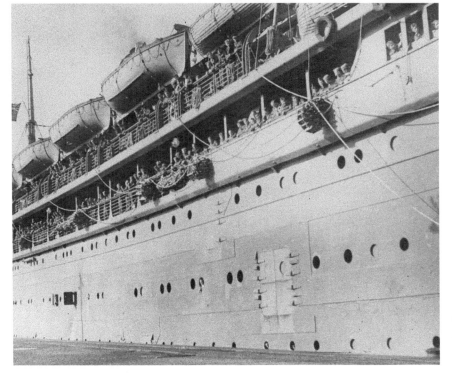

The SS *Rangitiki* arrives at Cardiff Docks, November 1942.

The CT-71 tug boat being discharged from the SS *Imperial*.

The hospital ship *Atlantis* visited Cardiff Docks in July 1943.

A mobile crane in action at Alexandra Dock, March 1944.

General cargo vessels in Queen Alexandra Dock, August 1945.

Troops aboard the *Santa Paula*, November 1943.

Another ship that visited Cardiff Docks in November 1943 was the SS *Espana Bay*.

The SS *Deseado* at King's Wharf Cold Stores, March 1944.

The *Efploia* and *Myron* berthed at Cardiff Docks, *c.*1973.

Mercantile Pioneer, Cardiff Docks, *c.*1960.

Lucellum Liverpool in Roath Dock, *c.*1960.

The *Alexander T. Wood* arriving at Cardiff Docks with 19,500 tons of iron ore, the largest cargo of iron ore to be discharged at the port, February 1962.

These gliders packed in cases are loaded on to the SS *Empire Freetown*.

During World War Two gliders for the Eastern Mediterranean were shipped from Cardiff Docks.

Government stores awaiting shipment at Cardiff Docks, August 1945.

US army vehicles await shipment at Cardiff Docks, August 1945.

Cardiff Docks had its own cattle lairs and stables.

Goods awaiting shipment at Cardiff Docks during World War Two.

British Steel Corporation works.

As long ago as 1891 steel was being made in Cardiff.

Guest Keen and Nettlefolds steel works rolling mill at Tremorfa.

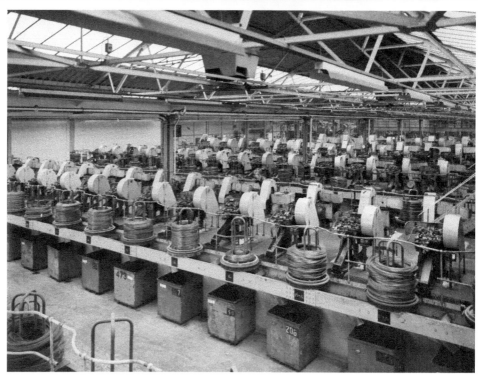

The nail factory at Tremorfa produced 800 tons of nails a week.

Built around 1890, these warehouses had been out of use when this picture was taken.

Some warehouses, like this one, were converted into hotels.

Alexandra Warehouse.

Warehouses are being replaced by luxury flats and houses in the Dock's area of Cardiff.

The date on the top of this old warehouse reads 1867.

A sad scene of dereliction.

A deserted docklands.

Bute Road. The Salvation Army Men's Hostel is left of picture, *c.*1950.

Pleasure boats in Cardiff Bay.

The five-star St David's Hotel.

One of the few remaining buildings is the historic Pierhead Building.

CHAPTER SIX

CARDIFF BAY

In 1987, the Cardiff Bay Development Corporation was set up to regenerate the Cardiff docks area, which had become a scene of dereliction. Twenty years on and the area has been transformed and is now home to the £106 million Wales Millennium Centre, the National Assembly of Wales building and the Glamorgan County Offices. Thousands of new homes and luxury apartments have been built and cinemas, shops, restaurants, cafés and other places of entertainment attract Cardiffians and tourists alike. The newly opened commerical businesses also provide work for thousands.

A major industrial landmark – the East Moors Steelworks – was demolished in 1979.

The company that had the task of demolition was Bird Brothers of Chepstow.

These stacks went down without any trouble, but it took a number of explosions to demolish the washery.

The blast furnaces at East Moors. Production had ceased on 28 April 1978.

The blast furnaces are demolished, and the workmen (left of picture) examine their 'handiwork'.

Business parks and workshops are now situated on the site.

A workman takes cover as the last of the chimney stacks is demolished.

An aerial photograph of Cardiff Bay.

The Rover Works.

Rubbish tips at Ferry Road.

Ferry Road looking north-east.

The inner harbour at high tide.

Bailey Dry Dock.

The Cogan Spur.

The River Ely at high tide.

Penarth Marina.

Luxury flats and marine buildings at Penarth.

The River Ely at low tide.

The environment tip at Cardiff Bay.

Wales Millennium Centre.

Cardiff Bay today.

Bute Road railway bridge. The Glastonbury Arms was established in 1889.

The new houses in Angelina Street.

Windsor Esplanade.

Around the Coal Exchange Building.

The Coal Exchange, which is being converted into luxury flats.

The façade of the Coal Exchange.

Boston Building in James Street.

The South Glamorgan County Hall.

Baltic House.

Flats replaced the old houses in Louisa Place.

Pleasure boats in Cardiff Bay.

East Moors Steel Works before demolition.

Thousands of tourists are attracted to Cardiff Bay every year.

The popular Esplanade Hotel in Penarth, which was destroyed in a fire.

Spillers and Bakers. A docks landmark for generations of Cardiffians.

The Spillers and Bakers warehouse was converted into luxury apartments in 1988.

Caronia school ship, *c*.1970

*Cardiff Queen, c.*1970.

The *Westgarth* tug, *c.*1970.

A P&A *Campbell* steamer gets a facelift, *c.*1970.

The damaged *Galway* in dock for repairs, *c.*1970.

*Methane Pioneer, c.*1970.

*Glen Usk, c.*1970.

A badly damaged *Clyde Explorer* after a collision at sea, *c.*1970.

The *Duchess of Normandy, c.*1970.

The *Loyal Celt* tug boat. Penarth Head can be seen to the right of the picture, *c.*1970.

The *Desponia* and *Loyal Celt* (foreground), *c.*1970.

The *Geest Bay*, *c.*1970.

Timber boat *List*, *c*.1970.

Ely dredger, *c*.1970.

*St Trillo, c.*1970.

A general dock scene, *c.*1970.

The Royal Yacht *Britannia*, July 1969.

Another view of the *Methane Pioneer*, *c.*1970.

CHAPTER SEVEN

EAST MOORS LINK ROAD

The Peripheral Distributor Road (PDR) provided access to the principal industrial areas from the M4 in the west and east and gave each sector of Cardiff its own access to a primary road system. This significantly reduced traffic, particularly commercial vehicles, on the city's existing roads and so improved road safety, public transport and the environment. Access was also improved to the Vale of Glamorgan, Barry Docks and Cardiff (Wales) Airport.

The official notice for the Peripheral Distributor Road (East Moors Link Phase 2) was placed near the River Rhymney Bridge.

Work is commenced. Planning permission was granted on 19 June 1980.

The PDR was built to provide improved access to the main industrial areas from the M4 and to give Cardiff its own access to a primary road system.

The columns were cast using a special shutter.

Shephard Hill Ltd
appointed Robert
Benaim & Associates
to carry out the design
of the permanent
works.

The segments were cast on site.

Workers inspecting one of the segments.

The high-quality smooth finish of the segments contrasted with the ribbed finish of the overhanging sections.

An almost completed segment, June 1984.

A viaduct section carries the road over the River Rhymney at two points as well as over the main London to Cardiff railway line.

Pre-cast deck units were manufactured in a purpose-built factory on site.

The project was financed by South Glamorgan County Council with grants from the Welsh office and European Regional Development Fund.

Almost there! June 1984.

An exceptionally high degree of supervision and control of pre-casting was required.

The bridge deck is a prestressed concrete trapezoidal box girder with side cantilevers.

To aid future maintenance inspections, a lockable steel access door is situated at each abutment.

There is also fluorescent lighting through the inside of the bridge deck.

On the inside of the bridge deck there are frequent power points.

The 950-metre long, three-lane viaduct consists of 15 52-metre, one 44-metre and two 41-metre long spans.

The carriageway for the length of the viaduct is 10 metres wide, reverting to a conventional 7.3-metre wide dual carriageway on the embankment and roundabout entry.

The viaduct has a vertical curve to gain sufficent height over the Newport Road roundabout and railway lines and is 'S' shaped.

A view of Newport Road taken from the viaduct. The historic pottery can be seen right of picture.

The main Cardiff rail link.

The total length of the viaduct is 913.5 metres in 18 spans, supported by 17 pairs of columns and two abutments.

A section of the PDR, which crosses over the River Rhymney at two points.

The tower of St Augustine's Church can be seen to the right of this picture showing houses in Rumney.

Another section of the PDR, photographed in 1984.

CHAPTER EIGHT
AROUND AND ABOUT

It was in 1849 that work commenced on the diverting of the course of the River Taff, which then ran along Westgate Street. Completed in 1853, this new cut reduced the risk of flooding in the city centre.

Cardiff Bridge, the main bridge over the River Taff, often mistakenly called Canton Bridge, was widened in 1931. The original mediaeval timbered bridge was replaced by a stone bridge in 1552. Several bridges built later could not withstand the storms and floods and the town bridge was rebuilt in 1859 and widened in 1877. The present widened bridge was opened by the Marchioness of Bute in 1931. The Glamorgan Canal was excavated between 1790 and 1798. Some 25 miles long, it ran from Merthyr to Cardiff and was built to bring iron and coal down from the valleys to Cardiff Docks.

In 2007 the industrial site off Colchester Avenue was being razed to the ground to prepare the land for a housing estate. The Cardiff Power Station, seen in this chapter, was built in 1902 and closed in 1970, but it was not until 1972 that the cooling towers shown were demolished.

The Taff Vale Railway Station was opened in 1840 and ran between Cardiff and Abercynon. The following year the line was extended to Merthyr Tydfil and it is now known as the Queen Street Railway Station.

When the River Taff ran through Westgate Street.

Westgate Street. Jackson Hall
is right of picture, *c.*1880.

Entrance to the Taff Vale Railway Station, now Queen Street Station, *c.*1880.

A pre-World War One view of the old bridge spanning the River Ely.

15083 NORTH ROAD IN WINTER.

A Christmas card scene showing one of the 52 locks of the Glamorgan Canal, which opened in 1794.

The toll gate at Penarth Road.

Only the façade of St David's Hospital, once known as the Canton Union Workhouse, remains, c.1920.

Canton Municipal Secondary School, which later became Canton High School, *c.*1920.

A snowy Cowbridge Road East in around 1910.

Still snowing in
Cowbridge Road East,
only this time in 1947.

Pope's sweet shop in Cowbridge Road East. Mr Pope (in window) is pictured with his family, *c.*1910.

Pope's sweet shop in around 1930.

The butcher's shop Alfred Lougher
& Son Ltd was situated at 156
Cowbridge Road East in 1964.

Forty years later Johnsons the dry cleaners and Klick Photoprint had taken over the premises of Alfred Lougher & Sons Ltd the butcher in Cowbridge Road East.

Deri Farm, Roath, which was situated near Penylan Road, c.1890.

Grange Farm, in Cathays, was at the west end of Llantrisant Street, *c*.1890.

Children gather around the photographer at Grange Farm, seen from a different angle, *c*.1890.

Highcroft Farm, Newport Road, Rumney, *c.*1950. A police station was built near the site.

Rumney Bridge looking towards the town, *c.*1909.

Western Avenue Bridge, Gabalfa, was opened to traffic in 1933.

Leckwith Bridge was opened in 1935.

Another view of Leckwith Bridge, 1935.

A tram crosses Clarence Road Bridge, which was opened by the Duke of Clarence in 1890.

The Cardiff Power Station in Colchester Avenue was built in 1902 and closed in 1970.

The building on the right-hand side of the picture is the BBC Wales television and radio studios at Llandaff, 1967.

Grange Farm, Clive Street, Grangetown, 1890.

Sophia Gardens
Pavilion, built for
the 1951 Festival
of Britain and
closed in 1981
when the roof
caved in after a
heavy snowstorm.

Mill Lane open-air market in the 1960s. It moved to a new site in Bridge Street in 1981.

Charles Street. St David's Roman Catholic Cathedral, which was gutted by fire caused by Nazi incendiary bombs in 1941, is left of picture.

Midland Bank, Broadway. The shop next door is Bollom the dry cleaners, c.1936.

F.W. Woolworth & Co., Clifton Street, Broadway, *c.* 1936.

O' Dare's kiosk, which used to be on the junction of Sloper Road and Leckwith Road, *c.*1936.

The Pump House in Penarth Road, *c.*1930. It is now an antiques centre.

The junction of City Road, Crwys Road and Albany Road, where the Catholic priests Father Phillip Evans and Father John Lloyd were executed in 1679, when the area was known as Gallows Fields.

Brownhill's Garage in North Road was situated almost opposite Maindy Stadium, c.1936.

CHAPTER NINE
SPORT AND LEISURE

Maindy Stadium is now known as Maindy Pool, and the running track on which the late John Tarrant set a new world best of four hours three minutes and 28 seconds for the 40-mile track event in 1966 and on which Welshman Lynn Hughes was to later become the first to break the four-hour barrier has long been dug up. Only the cycle track remains, along with a swimming pool. Another Mecca of Welsh sport that has vanished is the world-famous Cardiff Arms Park, which was replaced by the Millennium Stadium. Also vanished is the Empire Swimming Pool, which was popular with thousands of swimmers but had to be demolished to make way for the Millennium Stadium.

Maindy Pool, which claimed the lives of a number of adults and children and on which Maindy Stadium was built, 27 August 1928.

Workers building the stands of Maindy Stadium with stones from the banks of the Glamorgan Canal.

The cycle track, which was said to be one of the best in the world at the time, is completed in 1950.

The first athletics meeting was staged in 1951 and drew a tremendous crowd.

The stand seen in the following picture was not completed when this picture was taken.

A schools athletics meeting. Now both the stand and running track have disappeared.

The start of the 1958 Welsh AAA Marathon. Tommy Wood (Newport Harriers) leads Rhys Davies (Coventry Codiva), Ron Franklyn (Newport Harriers), Ken Flowers (Hereford Light Infantry) and author Brian Lee (Roath Cardiff Harriers). Davies won in two hours 35 minutes and 29 seconds.

The changing rooms at Maindy Stadium, which have now been demolished.

Author Brian Lee being interviewed by BBC Wales's Frank Hennessy at Maindy Stadium in 1999. The running track on which Brian trained has disappeared.

Wales' Empire Pool, which was built for the 1958 Empire and Commonwealth Games.

Built at a cost of around £700,000, the Empire Pool was the city's first championship-sized swimming pool.

It was a great shame when the Empire Pool was demolished as it was popular with thousands of swimmers.

The Empire Pool had seating for 2,400 spectators.

Taking a plunge! The restaurant can be seen in the background.

The entrance to the once world-famous Cardiff Arms Park, Westgate Street, c.1950.

Entrance to the Cardiff Arms Park cricket ground, Westgate Street, *c*.1950. County Championships were played here until 1967 when Glamorgan played at their new home at Sophia Gardens.

Greyhound racing (note advertisement left of picture) took place at the Cardiff Arms Park from 1928 until 1977.

Fred Trevillion's *Trev's Perfection* won the 1947 Welsh Greyhound Derby at Cardiff Arms Park and this picture shows Mr Trevillion (second right) with former famous boxer Jimmy Wilde and racing manager John Hegarty holding the winners' trophy.

Rugby writer John Billot described the 1957 Wales against Ireland international as 'a gruelling mudlark'. The entire Welsh team were ordered off the field after just 17 minutes to change their jerseys! Wales won by six points to five.

French forward J.P. Saux battles his way through a loose maul, with D.O. Brace (Wales) waiting to tackle him. France won by 16 points to 8. 26 March 1960.

Cardiff boxer Malcolm Collins had the honour of carrying the Welsh flag at the 1958 Empire and Commonwealth Games, Cardiff Arms Park. Author Brian Lee (arms folded) can be seen to the right of him.

The opening ceremony of the 1958 Empire and Commonwealth Games.

Motorcycle speedway racing first came to Cardiff at the Sloper Road Stadium (1928–37). This picture shows the new purpose-built stadium at Penarth Road (1951–53).

The roar of the motorbikes, the smell of the fuel and the clouds of shale dust thrown up as the riders rounded a bend made it all very exciting.

Generations of Cardiffians enjoyed a swim in Llandaff Fields open-air swimming baths.

The baths were shut down in the 1990s and filled in with rubble from a demolished farmhouse in the area.

Before World War Two, Cardiff's Ely Racecourse (1855–1939) used to attract thousands of racegoers from all over the country.

Youngsters enjoying a splash at Victoria Park, c.1950.

Victoria Park was the home of the legendary Billy the Seal from 1912 until 1939.

Roath Park Lake in the 1950s when swimming was allowed. Note the diving board on the far side.

In 1915 the Captain Scott memorial lighthouse was erected and it is seen here in 2003.

Roath Park Lake by night, 2005. More than 50 species of wildfowl can be found in the park.

The National Museum of Wales, *c*.1953. It attracts thousands of tourists each year.

Cardiff Castle is the capital city of Wales's main attraction, *c.*1920.

A pretty little park right in the civic centre is Friary Gardens. The statue of the third Marquis of Bute was unveiled in 1930.

Another park in the civic centre is Alexandra Gardens. In the background is the University of Wales building, *c.*1920.

The druid stones in Gorsedd Gardens with the City Hall and clock tower in the background, *c.*1920.

ND - #0362 - 270225 - C0 - 260/195/12 - PB - 9781780913339 - Gloss Lamination